Getting Off Track

*The Hoover Institution gratefully acknowledges
the generous support of*

PRESTON AND CAROLYN BUTCHER

Getting Off Track

How Government Actions and Interventions Caused, Prolonged, and Worsened the Financial Crisis

by JOHN B. TAYLOR

HOOVER INSTITUTION PRESS
| Stanford University | Stanford, California |

The Hoover Institution on War, Revolution and Peace, founded at Stanford University in 1919 by Herbert Hoover, who went on to become the thirty-first president of the United States, is an interdisciplinary research center for advanced study on domestic and international affairs. The views expressed in its publications are entirely those of the authors and do not necessarily reflect the views of the staff, officers, or Board of Overseers of the Hoover Institution.

www.hoover.org

Hoover Institution Press Publication No. 570

Hoover Institution at Leland Stanford Junior University, Stanford, California, 94305-6010

First printing 2009
16 15 14 13 12 11 10 09   9 8 7 6 5 4 3

Manufactured in the United States of America

This book is printed on acid-free paper.

Library of Congress Cataloging-in-Publication Data
Taylor, John B.
   Getting off track : how government actions and interventions caused, prolonged, and worsened the financial crisis / by John B. Taylor.
      p.   cm. — (Hoover Institution Press publication series ; no. 570)
   Includes bibliographical references and index.
   ISBN 978-0-8179-4971-6 (hardback : alk. paper)
   1. Financial crises.   2. Financial crises—United States.
3. Monetary policy.   4. Mortgages—Government policy.
I. Hoover Institution Press.   II. Title.
HB3722.T39   2009
330.973—dc22   2009003410

To Allyn

Contents

List of Figures

Preface

WHAT CAUSED THE FINANCIAL CRISIS? What prolonged it? What worsened it dramatically more than a year after it began? Rarely in economics is there a single answer to such questions, but the empirical research I present in this book strongly suggests that specific government actions and interventions should be first on the list of answers to all three. I focus on the period from the start of the crisis through the fall of 2008, when market conditions deteriorated precipitously and rapidly. Simply put, when policy started getting off track—especially when compared with the period of good performance during the previous two decades—financial and economic conditions turned sour.

This book integrates a series of research papers, speeches at central banks, and congressional testimony I have written on the financial crisis during the past two years. That work is detailed in the reference section at the end of the book; bracketed numbers in the text refer to the specific works. I have used empirical evidence to the extent possible and explained the analysis in the easy-to-understand terms, employing a series of illustrative graphs. I first integrated this research into a simple, short, yet comprehensive analysis of the crisis in the keynote lecture I was asked to give at a conference in Ottawa in honor of David Dodge, former governor of the Bank of Canada and a close friend whom I worked with in government for many years. Following that conference I circulated a written version of the lecture to colleagues who reacted positively to the novelty of the conclusions and the clarity of the explanations and stressed the importance of telling the story more widely. With the encouragement of John Raisian, director of the Hoover Institution, and George Shultz, distinguished fellow at the Hoover Institution, I decided to publish this book.

The first three chapters address the three questions raised above and are based on the David Dodge Lecture. Two additional chapters provide perspective and deeper background on some essential issues. Chapter 4, adapted from a speech I gave in Spain in the summer of 2007 before the crisis flared up, provides perspective by reviewing episodes in the previous twenty years when things went right. Chapter 5, based on a research paper I wrote with John Williams, director of research at the Federal Reserve Bank of San Francisco, shows how we diagnosed—in real time—that the problems in the financial markets that flared up in 2007 were due to counterparty risk rather than liquidity. The Epilogue draws policy implications and is followed by Frequently Asked Questions that have been raised about the analysis and findings during the course of the research.

1

What Caused the Financial Crisis

THE CLASSIC EXPLANATION OF FINANCIAL CRISES, going back hundreds of years, is that they are caused by excesses—frequently monetary excesses—that lead to a boom and an inevitable bust. In the recent crisis we had a housing boom and bust, which in turn led to financial turmoil in the United States and other countries. I begin by showing that monetary excesses were the main cause of that boom and the resulting bust.

Loose-Fitting Monetary Policy

Figure 1 was published in *The Economist* magazine in October 2007 as a simple way to illustrate the story of monetary excesses. The figure is based on a paper [1] that I presented at the annual Jackson Hole conference at which central bankers from around the world assembled in August 2007. It examines

Federal Reserve policy decisions—in terms of the federal funds interest rate—from 2000 to 2006.

The line that dips down to 1 percent in 2003, stays there into 2004, and then rises steadily until 2006 shows the actual interest-rate decisions of the Federal Reserve. The other line shows what the interest rate would have been had the Fed followed the type of policy that it had followed fairly regularly during the previous twenty-year period of good economic performance. *The Economist* labels that line the Taylor rule because it is a smoothed version of the interest rate one gets by plugging actual inflation and gross domestic product (GDP) into the policy rule that I proposed in 1992. When he was president of the Federal Reserve Bank of St. Louis, William Poole presented a similar chart, covering a longer period and without the smoothing, in an essay called "Understanding the Fed," published in the Federal Reserve Bank of St. Louis *Review* in 2007. The important point is that this line shows what the interest rate would have been had the Fed followed the kind of policy that had worked well during the period of economic stability called the Great Moderation, which began in the early 1980s.

Figure 1 shows that the actual interest-rate decisions fell well below what historical experience would suggest policy should be. It thus provides an empirical measure that monetary policy was too easy during this period, or too "loose fitting," as *The Economist* puts it. This deviation of monetary policy from the Taylor rule was unusually large; no greater or more persistent deviation of actual Fed policy had been seen since the turbulent days of the 1970s. This is clear evidence of monetary excesses during the period leading up to the housing boom.

Loose fitting

Federal funds rate, actual and counterfactual, (in percent)

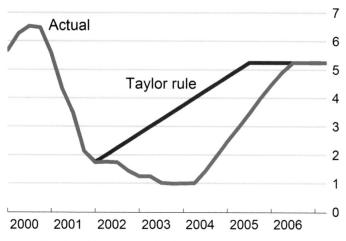

FIGURE 1. Chart from *The Economist*, October 18, 2007

The unusually low interest-rate decisions were, of course, made with careful consideration by monetary policy makers. One could interpret them as purposeful deviations from the "regular" interest-rate settings based on the usual macroeconomic variables. The Fed used transparent language to describe the decisions, saying, for example, that interest rates would be low for "a considerable period" and that they would rise slowly at a "measured pace," ways of clarifying that the decisions were deviations from the rule in some sense. Those actions were thus essentially discretionary government interventions in that they deviated from the regular way of conducting policy in order to address a specific problem, in particular a fear of deflation, as had occurred in Japan in the 1990s.

The Counterfactual: No Boom, No Bust

In presenting this chart to the central bankers in Jackson Hole in the late summer of 2007, I argued that this extra-easy policy accelerated the housing boom and thereby ultimately led to the housing bust. Others had made similar arguments. *The Economist* magazine wrote, in the issue then on the newsstands, that, "by slashing interest rates (by more than the Taylor rule prescribed) the Fed encouraged a house-price boom."

To support the argument empirically, I provided statistical evidence showing that the interest-rate deviation in Figure 1 could plausibly bring about a housing boom. I did this by using regression techniques to estimate a model of the empirical relationship between the interest rate and housing starts; I then simulated that model to see what would have happened in the counterfactual event that policy had followed the rule in Figure 1. In this way I provided empirical proof that monetary policy was a key cause of the boom and hence the bust and the crisis.

Figure 2 summarizes the results of this empirical approach. It is a picture of housing starts in the United States during the same period as Figure 1; it is drawn from that same 2007 Jackson Hole paper. The jagged line shows actual housing starts in millions of units. Both the housing boom and the housing bust are clear in this picture.

The line labeled "counterfactual" in Figure 2 is what a statistically estimated model of housing starts suggests would have happened had interest rates followed the rule in Figure 1; clearly there would have not been such a big housing boom and bust. Hence, Figure 2 provides empirical evidence that the unusually low interest-rate policy was a factor in the housing

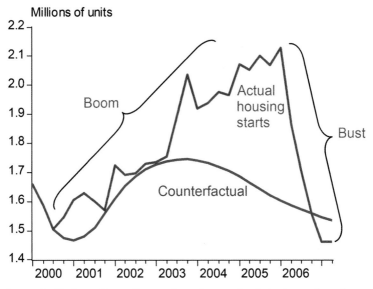

Figure 2. The Boom-Bust in Housing Starts Compared with the Counterfactual

boom. One can challenge this conclusion, of course, by challenging the model, but by using a model and an empirical counterfactual, one has a formal framework for debating the issue.

Not shown in Figure 2 is the associated boom and bust in housing prices in the United States. The boom-bust was evident throughout most of the country but was worse in California, Florida, Arizona, and Nevada. The exceptions were in states such as Texas and Michigan, where local factors offset the monetary excess stressed here.

Although the housing boom was the most noticeable effect of the monetary excesses, the effects could also be seen in more gradually rising overall prices: inflation based on the consumer price index (CPI), for example, averaged 3.2 percent annually

during the past five years, well above the 2 percent target suggested by many policy makers and implicit in the policy rule
in Figure 1. It is always difficult to predict the exact initial impacts of monetary shocks, but housing was also a volatile part
of GDP in the 1970s, another period of monetary instability
before the onset of the Great Moderation. The more systematic monetary policy followed during the Great Moderation
had the advantages of keeping both the overall economy stable and the inflation rate low.

Competing Explanations: A Global Saving Glut

Some argue that the low interest rates in 2002–4 were caused
by global factors beyond the control of the monetary authorities. If so, then the interest-rate decisions by the monetary authorities were not the major factor causing the boom. This
explanation—appealing at first glance because long-term interest rates remained low for a while after the short-term federal funds rate began increasing—focuses on global saving. It
argues that there was an excess of world saving—a global saving glut—that pushed interest rates down in the United States
and other countries.

The main problem with this explanation is that there is no
actual evidence of a global saving glut. On the contrary, as Figure 3 shows in simple terms, there seems to have been a saving shortage. This figure, produced by staff at the International
Monetary Fund in 2005, shows that the global saving rate—
world saving as a fraction of world GDP—was low in the
2002–4 period, especially when compared with the 1970s and
1980s. Thus, this explanation does not stand up to empirical
testing using data that have long been available.

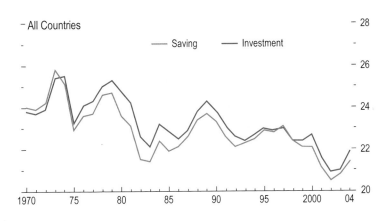

FIGURE **3.** Global Saving and Investment as a Share of World GDP (in percent)
Source: *World Economic Outlook*, International Monetary Fund, Sept. 2005, Chapter 2, p. 92.

To be sure, there was a gap of saving over investment in the world *outside* the United States during 2002–4, which may be the source of the term *saving glut*. But the United States was saving less than it was investing during this period; it was running a current account deficit, implying that saving was less than investment. Thus, the positive saving gap outside the United States was offset by an equal-sized negative saving gap in the United States. No extra impact on world interest rates would be expected. As implied by simple global accounting, there is no global gap between saving and investment.

Monetary Policy in Other Countries: Central Banks Looking at Each Other?

Nevertheless there are possible global connections to keep track of when assessing the root cause of the crisis. Most important is the evidence that interest rates at several other central banks also deviated from what historical regularities, as described by the Taylor rule, would predict. Even more striking is that housing booms were largest where the deviations from the rule were largest. Three economists at the Organization for Economic Cooperation and Development (OECD), Rudiger Ahrend, Boris Cournède, and Robert Price, provide a fascinating analysis of the experiences in OECD countries during this period in their working paper, "Monetary Policy, Market Excesses and Financial Turmoil," of March 2008. They show that the deviations from the Taylor rule explain a large fraction of the cross-country variation in housing booms in OECD countries. For example, within Europe the deviations from the Taylor rule vary in size because inflation and output data vary from country to country. The country with the largest deviation from the rule, Spain, had the biggest housing boom, measured by the change in housing investment as a share of GDP. The country with the smallest deviation, Austria, had the smallest change in housing investment as a share of GDP. That close correlation is shown in Figure 4, which is drawn from their OECD working paper. It plots the sum of deviations from the policy rule on the horizontal axis and the change in housing investment as a share of GDP on the vertical axis from 2001 to 2006.

One important question, with implications for reforming the international financial system, is whether the low interest rates at other central banks were influenced by the decisions in the United States or represented an interaction among central banks that caused global short-term interest rates to be lower than they otherwise would have been. To test this hypothesis, I examined the decisions at the European Central Bank (ECB) in a paper [2] prepared for a talk in Europe in June 2007. I studied the deviations of the ECB's interest-rate deci-

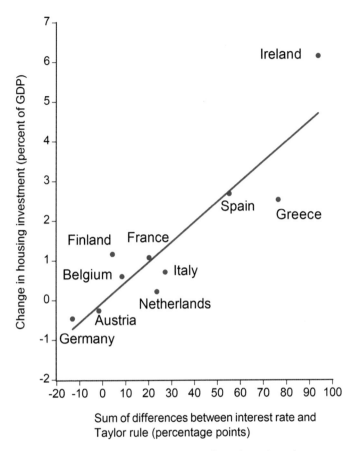

FIGURE 4. Housing Investment versus Deviations from the Taylor Rule in Europe During 2001–6

sions from the same type of policy rule as in Figure 1 but with Euro-zone inflation and GDP data. The interest rate set by the ECB was also below the rule; in other words, there were negative deviations. To determine whether those deviations were influenced by the Federal Reserve's interest-rate decisions, I examined the statistical relation between them during 2000–2006 and the federal funds rate shown in Figure 1. I found that the effect of the federal funds rate was statistically significant.

Figure 5 shows how much of the ECB's interest-rate decisions could be explained by the Fed's interest-rate decisions. It appears that a good fraction can be explained in this way. The jagged-looking line in Figure 5 demonstrates the deviations of the actual interest rates set by the ECB from the policy rule. (I have not smoothed out the high-frequency jagged movements as was done in Figure 1.) By this measure, the ECB interest rate was as much as 2 percentage points too low during this period. The smoother line shows that a good fraction of the deviation can be "explained" by the federal funds rate in the United States.

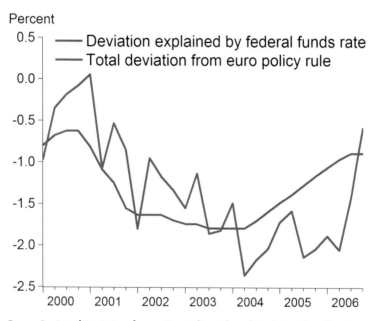

FIGURE 5. Actual Deviations from a Euro Policy Rule and Deviations Based on the Federal Funds Rate

The reasons for this connection are not clear from this statistical analysis, and they are a fruitful subject for future research. Indeed it is difficult to distinguish statistically between the ECB following the Fed and the Fed following the ECB; similar statistical analyses show that there is also a connection the other way, from the ECB to the Fed. Concerns about the exchange rate, or the influence of the exchange rate on inflation, could generate such a relationship, as could third factors, such as changes in the global real interest rate.

Monetary Interaction with the Subprime Mortgage Problem

A sharp boom and bust in the housing markets would be expected to affect the financial markets, as falling house prices led to delinquencies and foreclosures. Those effects were amplified by several complicating factors, including the use of subprime mortgages, especially the adjustable-rate variety, which led to excessive risk taking. In the United States such risk taking was encouraged by government programs designed to promote home ownership, a worthwhile goal but overdone in retrospect. During 2003–5, when short-term interest rates were still unusually low, the number of adjustable-rate mortgages (ARMs) rose to about one-third of total mortgages and remained at that high level for an unusually long time. This made borrowing attractive and brought more people into the housing markets, further bidding up housing prices.

It is important to note, however, that the excessive risk taking and the low-interest monetary policy decisions are connected. Evidence for this connection is shown in Figure 6, which plots housing price inflation along with foreclosure and delinquency rates on adjustable-rate subprime mortgages. The figure shows the sharp increase in housing price inflation from mid 2003 to early 2006 and the subsequent decline. Observe how delinquency rates and foreclosure rates were inversely related to housing price inflation during this period. In the years of rapidly rising housing prices, delinquency and foreclosure rates declined rapidly. The benefits of holding onto a house, perhaps by working longer hours to make the payments, are higher when the price of the house is rapidly rising. When prices are falling, the incentives to make payments are much less and turn negative if the price of the house falls below the value of the mortgage. Hence, delinquencies and foreclosures rise.

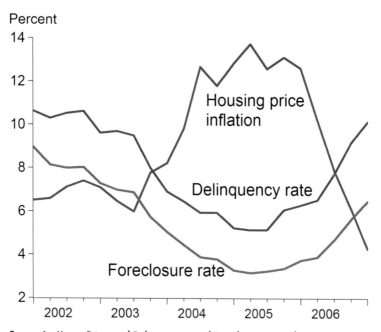

FIGURE 6. House Prices and Delinquencies and Foreclosures on Subprime Adjustable-Rate Mortgages

Mortgage underwriting procedures are supposed to take into account actual foreclosure rates and delinquency rates in cross-section data. Those procedures, however, would have been overly optimistic during the period when prices were rising unless they took into account the time series correlation in Figure 6. Thus, there is an interaction between the monetary excesses and the risk-taking excesses. This illustrates how unintended things can happen when policy deviates from the norm. In this case, the rapidly rising housing prices and the resulting low delinquency rates likely threw the underwriting programs off track and misled many people.

More Complications: Complex Securitization, Fannie, and Freddie

These problems were amplified because the adjustable-rate subprime and other mortgages were packed into mortgage-backed securities of great complexity. The rating agencies underestimated the risk of these securities because of a lack of competition, poor accountability, or, most likely, an inherent difficulty in assessing risk due to the complexity. These complex mortgage-backed securities led to what might be called the "Queen of Spades problem," as in the game of Hearts. In the game of Hearts, you don't know where the Queen of Spades is and you don't want to get stuck with it. The Queens of Spades—and there are many of them in the mortgage game—were the securities with the bad mortgages in them and people didn't know where they were. People didn't know which banks were holding them eighteen months ago, and they still don't know where they are. That risk in the balance sheets of financial institutions has been at the heart of the financial crisis from the beginning.

In the United States other government actions were at play. The government-sponsored agencies Fannie Mae and Freddie Mac were encouraged to expand and buy mortgage-backed securities, including those formed with the risky subprime mortgages. Although legislation, such as the Federal Housing Enterprise Regulatory Reform Act of 2005, was proposed to control those excesses, it was not passed into law. Thus the actions of those agencies should be added to the list of government interventions that were part of the problem.

2

What Prolonged the Crisis

THE FINANCIAL CRISIS became acute on August 9 and 10, 2007, when the money market interest rates rose dramatically. Figure 7 illustrates this using a measure that has since become the focus of many studies. That measure is the spread between the three-month London Inter-bank Offered Rate (Libor) and the three-month overnight index swap (OIS). The OIS is a measure of what the markets expect the federal funds rate to be over the three-month period comparable to the three-month Libor. Subtracting OIS from Libor effectively controls for expectations effects, which are a factor in all term loans, including the three-month Libor. The difference between Libor and OIS is thus due to things other than interest-rate expectations, such as risk and liquidity effects.

If you look at the lower left of Figure 7 you see a spread of about 10 basis points (0.1 percentage point). If you extended that to the left, you would see a similar level of about 10 basis points. On August 9 and 10, 2007, this spread jumped to

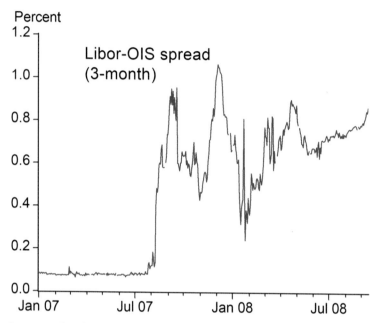

FIGURE 7. The Libor-OIS (overnight index swap) Spread during the First Year of Crisis

unusually high levels and has remained high ever since. In our research [3] on this episode, John Williams and I called the event "A Black Swan in the Money Market" because it appeared to be so unusual. Figure 7 focuses on the first year of the crisis; the worsening situation in September and October 2008 is covered in the next chapter.

In addition to being a measure of financial stress, the spread affects the transmission mechanism of monetary policy to the economy because trillions of dollars of loans and securities are indexed to Libor. An increase in the spread, holding the OIS constant, will increase the cost of such loans and have a contractionary effect on the economy. Bringing this spread down therefore became a major objective of monetary policy, as well as a measure of its success in dealing with the market turmoil.

Diagnosing the Problem: Liquidity or Counterparty Risk?

Diagnosing the reason for the increased spreads was essential, of course, to determining the necessary policy response. If it was a liquidity problem, then providing more liquidity by making discount window borrowing easier or opening new windows or facilities would be appropriate. But if the issue was counterparty risk, then a direct focus on the quality and transparency of the banks' balance sheets would be appropriate, by requiring more transparency, by dealing directly with the increasing number of mortgage defaults as housing prices fell, or by looking for ways to bring more capital into the banks and other financial institutions.

In the fall of 2007 John Williams and I embarked on what we thought would be an interesting and possibly policy-relevant research project [3] to examine the issue. We interviewed traders who deal in the interbank market and we looked for measures of counterparty risk. The idea that counterparty risk was the reason for the increased spreads made sense because it corresponded to the Queen of Spades theory and other explanations for uncertainty about banks' balance sheets. At the time, however, many traders and monetary officials thought it was mainly a liquidity problem.

To assess the issue empirically, we looked for measures of risk in those markets to see if they correlated with the spread. One good measure of risk is the difference between interest rates on unsecured and secured interbank loans of the same maturity. Examples of secured loans are government-backed repos (repurchase agreements) between banks. A repo is a form of loan where one bank sells government bonds to another bank but agrees to buy them back at a certain date in the future. Hence, the bonds become collateral for the loan. In other words the loan is secured. By subtracting the interest rate on repos from Libor, you could get a measure of risk. Using regression methods, we then looked for the impact of this measure of risk on the Libor spread and showed that it could explain much of the variation in the spread. Other measures of risk gave the same results.

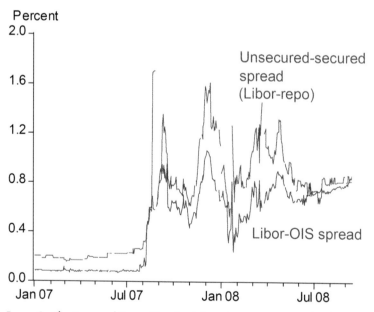

FIGURE 8. The Unsecured-Secured Interbank Loan Interest Rate Spread and the Libor-OIS Spread

The results are illustrated in Figure 8, which shows the high correlation between the unsecured-secured spread and the Libor-OIS spread. There seemed to be little, if any, role for liquidity. Those results suggested, therefore, that the market turmoil in the interbank market was not a liquidity problem of the kind that could be alleviated simply by central bank liquidity tools. Rather it was inherently a counterparty risk issue, which linked back to the underlying cause of the financial crisis. This was not a situation like the Great Depression, where just printing money or providing liquidity was the solution; rather the situation was due to fundamental problems in the financial sector relating to risk.

But this was not the diagnosis that drove economic policy during this period. Although it is difficult to determine policy makers' diagnoses because their rationales for their decisions are not always clearly explained, it appears that the increased spreads in the money markets were seen by the authorities as liquidity problems rather than risk problems. Accordingly, their early interventions focused on policies other than those that would deal with the fundamental sources of the heightened risk. As a result, in my view, the crisis continued.

As evidence I provide three examples of interventions that prolonged the crisis, either because they did not address the problem or because they had unintended consequences.

1. Term Auction Facility

To make it easier for banks to borrow from the Fed, the term auction facility (TAF) was introduced in December 2007.

With this new facility, banks could avoid going to the Fed's discount window; they could bid directly for funds from the Fed. Similar facilities were set up simultaneously at other central banks. The main aim of the TAF was to reduce the spreads in the money markets and thereby increase the flow of credit and lower interest rates. Figure 9, which is drawn from my paper with John Williams, shows the amount of funds taken up (on the right) along with the Libor-OIS spread (on the left). (Recall that this chart does not go beyond mid September 2008.)

Soon after the TAF was introduced in December 2007, the spread came down a bit, and some policy makers suggested that it was working. But soon the spread rose again. If you look at

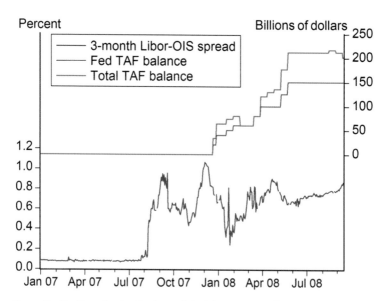

FIGURE 9. The Term Auction Facility and the Libor-OIS Spread

Figure 9, it is hard to see any effect on the spread during that period. This visual impression is confirmed with detailed statistical analysis. If the reason for the spread is seen as counterparty risk as distinct from liquidity, it is not surprising that the TAF did not make much difference.

2. Temporary Cash Infusions

Another early policy response was the Economic Stimulus Act of 2008, passed in February. The major part of this package consisted of sending checks totaling more than $100 billion to individuals and families in the United States; the rationale was that they would have more to spend and thus jump-start consumption and the economy. Most of the checks were sent in May, June, and July. Although not a purely monetary action because the rebate was financed by Treasury borrowing rather than money creation, like the liquidity facilities it did not focus on the underlying causes of the crisis.

Moreover, as would be predicted by the permanent income theory of consumption, people spent little if any of the temporary rebate, and thus consumption was not jump-started as had been hoped. The evidence is in Figure 10, which is drawn from research reported in "The State of the Economy and Principles for Fiscal Stimulus" [4]. The top line shows how personal disposable income jumped at the time of the rebate; the lower line shows that personal consumption expenditures did not increase in a noticeable way. As with the earlier charts, formal statistical work confirms the visual impression. It shows that the rebates caused no statistically significant increase in consumption.

Billions of dollars

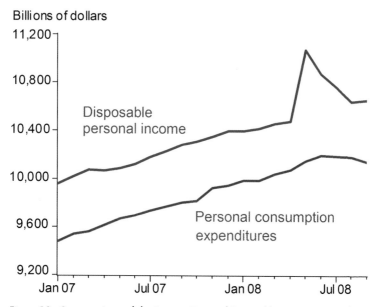

Figure 10. Consumption and the Jump in Personal Disposable Income Due to the Rebates. (Monthly data, seasonally adjusted, annual rates.)

3. The Initial Cuts in Interest Rates through April 2008

A third policy response to the financial crisis was the sharp reduction in the federal funds rate in the first half year of the crisis. The federal funds rate target went from 5.25 percent, when the crisis began in August 2007, to 2.0 percent in April 2008. Although the Taylor rule called for a reduction in the interest rate during this early period, it was not as sharp. Thus the reduction was more than would be called for using the historical relation stressed in Chapter 1, even adjusting for the Libor-OIS spread, as I suggested [5] in a speech at the Federal Reserve Bank of San Francisco and in testimony at the House Financial Services Committee in February.

It is difficult to assess the full impact of this extra-sharp easing, and more research is needed. The lower interest rates reduced the size of the reset of adjustable-rate mortgages and thereby addressed some of the fundamentals causing the crisis. Some of these effects would have occurred had the interest-rate cuts been less aggressive.

The most noticeable effects at the time of the cut in the federal funds rate, however, were the sharp depreciation of the dollar and the large rise in oil prices. During the first year of the financial crisis, oil prices doubled, from about $70 per barrel in August 2007 to more than $140 in July 2008, before plummeting back down as expectations of world economic growth declined sharply. Figure 11 shows the close correlation between

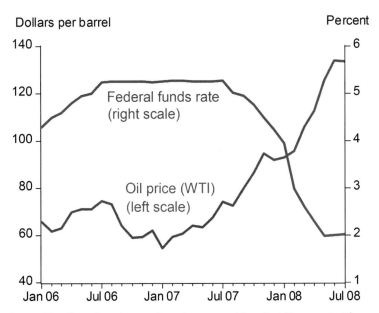

FIGURE 11. Sharp Cut in Interest Rates Accompanied by a Rapid Increase in Oil Prices through the First Year of the Crisis. (Last observation is July 2008.)

the federal funds rate and the price of oil during this period us-ing monthly average data (the chart ends before the global slump in demand became evident and oil prices fell back).

When the federal funds rate was cut, oil prices broke out of the $60–$70 per barrel range and then rose rapidly throughout the first year of the financial crisis. Clearly this bout of high oil prices hit the economy hard as gasoline prices skyrocketed and automobile sales plummeted in the spring and summer of 2008. In my view, expressed in a paper [6] delivered at the Bank of Japan in May, this interest-rate cut helped raise oil and other commodity prices and thereby prolonged the crisis.

Econometric evidence of the connection between interest rates and oil prices is found in existing empirical studies. For ex-ample, in early May 2008, the first deputy managing director of the International Monetary Fund, John Lipsky, said in a speech at the Council on Foreign Relations in New York: "Preliminary evidence suggests that low interest rates have a statistically sig-nificant impact on commodity prices, above and beyond the typical effect of increased demand. Exchange rate shifts also ap-pear to influence commodity prices. For example, IMF estimates suggest that if the US dollar had remained at its 2002 peak through end-2007, oil prices would have been $25 a barrel lower and non-fuel commodity prices 12 percent lower."

When it became clear in the fall of 2008 that the world economy was turning down sharply, oil prices then returned to the $60–$70 range. But by this time the damage from the high oil prices had been done.

3

Why the Crisis Worsened Dramatically a Year after it Began

FIGURE 12 SHOWS, using the same Libor-OIS measure of tension in the financial markets as in Figure 7, how dramatically the financial crisis worsened in October 2008. Recall that in our research paper on the subject, John Williams and I called the jump in spreads in August 2007 "A Black Swan in the Money Market." The October 2008 events were even more unusual. Not only was the crisis prolonged for more than a year, but it worsened, according to this measure, by a factor of four. It became a serious credit crunch with large spillovers, seriously weakening an economy already suffering from the lingering impacts of the high oil price bout and the housing bust. Notice the close correlation in Figure 12 between our measure of counterparty risk and the Libor-OIS spread, demonstrating convincingly that all along the problems in the market were related to risk rather than to liquidity.

Many commentators have argued that the crisis worsened because the U.S. government (specifically the Treasury and the

Percent

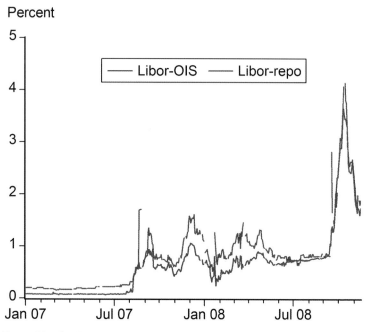

FIGURE 12. The Crisis Worsens

Federal Reserve) decided not to intervene to prevent the bankruptcy of Lehman Brothers over the weekend of September 13
and 14. It is difficult to bring a rigorous empirical analysis to this
important question, but researchers must do so because future
policy actions depend on the answer. Perhaps the best empirical analyses we can hope for at this time are event studies that
look carefully at reactions in the financial markets to various
decisions and events. Such an event study, summarized below,
suggests that the answer is more complicated than the decision
not to intervene to prevent the Lehman bankruptcy and, in my
view, lies elsewhere.

An Event Study

Figure 13 focuses on a few key events from September 1 through mid October—the last few observations in Figure 12. Since mid October a host of new policy interventions have taken place—including implementation of the Troubled Asset Relief Program (TARP), guarantees by the Federal Deposit Insurance Corporation (FDIC), Federal Reserve support for the commercial paper market, similar actions in other countries—and conditions have improved somewhat, as seen in the graph.

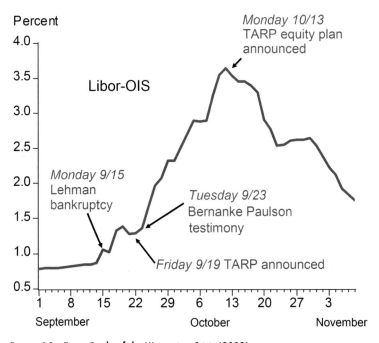

FIGURE 13. Event Study of the Worsening Crisis (2008)

But the question is, What led to the worsening conditions that have severely affected the economy and generated many unprecedented cleanup actions?

Recall that, for the year prior to the events in Figure 13, the spread had been fluctuating in the 50- to 100-basis-point range, which was where it was through the first half of September 2008. Note that the spread moved a bit on September 15, the Monday after the weekend decisions not to intervene in Lehman Brothers. It then bounced back down a little bit on September 16, around the time of the AIG intervention. Although the spread did rise during the week following the Lehman Brothers decision, it was not far out of line with the events of the previous year.

On Friday of that week, the Treasury announced that it was going to propose a large rescue package, though the size and details had not yet been determined. During the weekend the package was put together; on Tuesday, September 23, Federal Reserve Board Chairman Ben Bernanke and Treasury Secretary Henry Paulson testified at the Senate Banking Committee about the TARP, saying that it would be $700 billion in size. They provided a two-and-a-half-page legislation, with no mention of oversight and few restrictions on the use. During this testimony, they were questioned intensely, after which many members of Congress received a large volume of mail critical of Bernanke and Paulson's testimony. As shown in Figure 13 it was also following this testimony that the crisis began deepening, as measured by the relentless upward movement in the Libor-OIS spread over the next three weeks. As things steadily deteriorated, the spread went through the roof, to 3.5 percent.

No Predictable Framework for Intervention

The main message of Figure 13 is that identifying the decisions over the weekend of September 13 and 14 as the cause of the increased severity of the crisis is questionable; it was not until more than a week later that conditions deteriorated. Moreover, it is plausible that events around September 23 actually increased risks and drove the markets down, including the public's realization, shock, and fear that the intervention plan had not been fully thought through and that conditions were much worse than many had been led to believe. At a minimum a great deal of uncertainty about what the government would do to aid financial institutions, and under what circumstances, was revealed, thereby influencing business and investment decisions at the time. Such uncertainty would have driven up risk spreads in the interbank market and elsewhere. Some evidence of the uncertainty is found in a survey taken November 5 by the Securities Industry and Financial Markets Association (SIFMA), showing that 94 percent of securities firms and banks found the TARP lacking in clarity about its operations.

Uncertainties about the procedures or criteria for government intervention that would prevent financial institutions from failing had existed since the time of the Bear Stearns intervention in March. The implication of that decision for future interventions was not made clear by policy makers. This lack of predictability about Treasury-Fed intervention policy and recognition of the harm it could do to markets likely increased in the fall of 2008, when the underlying uncertainty was revealed for all to see. What was the rationale for intervening with Bear

Stearns, not intervening with Lehman, and then intervening again with AIG? What would guide the operations of the TARP?

Worries about the lack of clarity were raised in many quarters. At a conference on "The Future Role of Central Banking: The Urgent and Precedent-Setting Next Steps," held on the Stanford campus in July to address the new interventions, I argued [7] that the U.S. Treasury and the Fed urgently needed to develop a new framework for exceptional access to government support for financial institutions. I made analogies to a reform put in place at the IMF in 2003 that clarified the circumstances under which the IMF would provide loans to countries in crisis. After those IMF reforms were put in place, the eight-year emerging market crisis period that had begun in 1995 came to a close, events I explain more fully in Chapter 4.

Analogously, a new exceptional access framework would describe the process that the United States and other governments should take when intervening and providing loans to an institution. It would work like the IMF's exceptional access framework (EAF), the procedures the IMF should take when providing loans to a country. The more that policy makers could articulate the rationale and the procedures, the better.

4

What Went Right in the Two Decades before the Crisis

THE PREVIOUS THREE CHAPTERS explained how a series of unpredictable government actions and interventions with little or no basis in economic theory or experience threw the economy off track, increased uncertainty, and caused great economic harm—not a pleasant story. This chapter examines historical episodes in which policy moved toward a more predictable policy process based on clear economic principles and experience—and thereby greatly benefited many people.

Getting economic policy on track is never easy. I am reminded of the *Mission Impossible* TV and movie series: in one episode after another, people pursue a seemingly impossible mission and in the end the mission is, amazingly, accomplished. In this chapter, I examine three such missions impossible. The first—Mission Impossible I—began thirty years ago, the second—Mission Impossible II—began ten years ago, and the third—Mission Impossible III—just two years ago. For each mission, I discuss (1) the economic theory, or the ideas developed to accomplish the mission, (2) the policy, or the implementation of those ideas, and (3) the results. Unlike the movies, the connection between the theory, the policy, and the results is not obvious, but speculating about the connection is intriguing.

Mission Impossible I

Go back thirty years, to the mid to late 1970s. Inflation in the United States was into double digits and had been rising for a decade. The volatility of inflation was also high: as measured by the consumer price index (CPI), inflation reached 12 percent in 1975, fell to 5 percent in 1977, and then increased to 15 percent before the decade was over. Like inflation, the volatility of real GDP was high: the standard deviation of real GDP growth was about 3 percent, recessions came frequently, and expansions were short lived. According to National Bureau of Economic Research (NBER) dating, recessions occurred in 1969–70, 1973–75, 1980, and 1981–82, and some had chronicled another recession in 1977–78—a growth recession. Thus a recession took place about every three or four years. There seemed to be a connection between the fluctuations in real GDP and inflation: each time inflation rose to a new peak, it was followed by a recession, in boom-bust-cycle fashion.

There was also a global connection. The Bretton Woods fixed exchange-rate system had broken down in the early 1970s. Hence, central banks around the world were groping to find an alternative to the fixed exchange rate that had guided many of them in the past. The lack of a workable framework for monetary policy, fluctuations in the demand for money, and an incomplete understanding of the inflation-output trade-off created similar instabilities in inflation and output around the world. Large fluctuations in real GDP growth were as prevalent in other countries as in the United States.

It was also during the 1970s that economists—especially macroeconomists and monetary economists—began to focus explicitly on finding policies that could improve economic performance. Given the dismal macroeconomic conditions at the time, this intense policy focus was not surprising. Thus researchers began to talk about and use an explicit policy objective function in their research. The objective was to reduce the volatility of inflation and real GDP. Soon it was hard to find papers without a stated policy objective. The value of such an objective function was that it focused researchers on finding good policies.

Because the actual volatility of inflation and real GDP were very large at the time, the research seemed highly relevant and important. But it also seemed difficult, if not impossible, and hence the analogy with the dramatic opening of a *Mission Impossible* episode: "Your mission, should you choose to accept it, is to reduce inflation and output volatility around the world." The "you" in this challenge was the community of researchers and policy makers interested in and responsible for monetary policy—monetary economists both inside and outside central banks. Focused on the mission, they went about their research, bringing a vast array of new ideas to bear on the problem. They introduced a new method to model people's expectations—called the "rational expectations" method—into the macroeconomic models. They devised new theories about why inflation did not adjust rapidly after a change in monetary policy. They estimated the models empirically with new statistical techniques. They solved more and more complex models with new supercomputing methods, and they used mathematical techniques of stochastic control theory and dynamic programming to find the best policy. Many of the new research ideas—including the application of rational expectations—emphasized the importance of systematically formulating policy decisions as a policy rule rather than as a onetime path for the instruments.

Looking back, the amount of research output was amazing. But more amazing was that the mission was actually accomplished. As policy makers at the Federal Reserve and other central banks put the ideas into practice by explicitly stating their goals and formulating policy in a more systematic fashion, the variance of inflation and the variance of real GDP came down by a large amount. Compared to the recession-prone economy of the past, the United States went into a period where recessions occurred only once every eight years on average, far less frequently than once every three or four years. Only two recessions occurred in the twenty-five years from the end of the 1981–82 recession in the United States until 2007, and those two recessions were very short and mild by historical comparison. The standard deviation of real GDP growth was cut in half, to 1.5 percent. The reduction in volatility is clear in Figure 14.

Although this improvement, now called the Great Moderation or the Long Boom, began in the United States in the early 1980s, it was not until the 1990s that people began to document and study the decline in volatility of real GDP. The improvement did not only occur in the United States; similar improvements were seen in other developed countries around the world. The G7 countries as a whole, for example, cut the standard deviation of real GDP in half. Not until policy again went off track, as discussed in Chapter 1, did we seem to be leaving the Great Moderation behind.

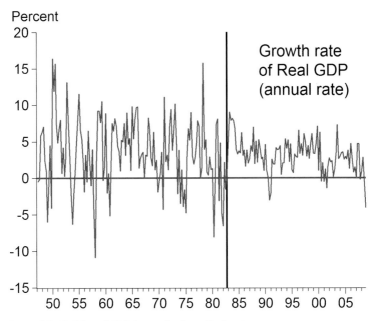

Percent

FIGURE 14. Stability of GDP during the Great Moderation

There is debate about the reasons for the improvements. I have argued that they were caused mainly by changes in monetary policy, implying that the mission was accomplished through more than luck alone. There is also debate about whether the research influenced the changes in monetary policy—about whether those ideas had actual consequences. At the Federal Reserve, the leadership of Paul Volcker and Alan Greenspan was essential to implementing the policies to getting inflation down and finding policies to keep it down. Indeed, Alan Greenspan once commented that the Fed deserved an "assist" in developing the Taylor rule. Although causality and influences are complex and difficult to prove, there is certainly a close relationship in time between the monetary research, the monetary policy, and the improvement in economic stability. Taking the Taylor rule as representative of the type of policy recommendation that emerged from the research, the improvement in economic performance occurred at about the same time that monetary policy began to follow such recommendations. Again this does not prove causation; indeed the timing is so close that two-way causation may be involved, although it is clear that the monetary policy rules were meant to be normative recommendations rather than simply descriptions of actual policy.

Those changes were global. The close correlation and timing between the greater adherence of actual policy to recommended policy rules and the better economic performance can be seen in many other countries, not only in the United States. The connection between the ideas, the policies, and the results are a global phenomenon that spread quickly around the world—another manifestation of globalization.

Mission Impossible II

For our second example we go to another place and another period of dismal economic performance: the period of crises in emerging market countries in the 1990s or, more precisely, from 1994 to 2002. Table 1 lists the large number of crises that occurred around the world during this period—beginning with the Mexican crisis in 1994 and the associated Tequila contagion, continuing onto the Asian crisis and its contagion, the Russian crisis and its contagion, and ending with Uruguay in 2002. Market crisis expert Guillermo Calvo aptly characterized the emerging market crises during this period: "Their frequency and global spread set them apart from anything else that we have seen—at least since World War II." The frequency and spread were so great and unusual that the period is better described as one eight-year financial crisis rather than eight years of financial crises.

Thousands of research papers have been written about this crisis period, many with the goal of better understanding and ultimately bringing an end to that period. Hence, again we have the analogy with the opening of a *Mission Impossible*

TABLE 1. The Eight-Year Emerging Market Crisis

The Beginning and the Tequila Contagion
   Mexico: 1994–95
   Argentina: 1995–96

The Asian Contagion
   Thailand: 1997–98
   Indonesia: 1997–98
   Malaysia: 1997–98
   Korea: 1997–98

The Russian Contagion
   Russia: 1998
   Brazil: 1998–2002
   Romania: 1998–99
   Ecuador: 1998–99
   Argentina: 1999–2001

The Ending
   Turkey: 2000–2001
   Uruguay: 2002

episode: "Your mission, should you choose to accept it, is to reduce the frequency and global spread of financial crises." The
challenge in Mission Impossible II was to the international
community of monetary and finance experts both inside and
outside of governments and central banks, with the International Monetary Fund (IMF) and its staff playing a much big-
ger role than in Mission Impossible I.

The End of the Eight-Year Crisis

Remarkably, similar to Mission Impossible I, this impossible
mission also seems to have become a mission accomplished. As

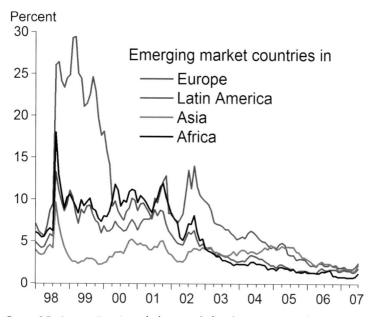

FIGURE 15. Interest Rate Spreads during and after the Emerging Market
Crisis Period

shown in Table 1, the period of emerging market financial crises and contagions of the kind we experienced regularly during the crisis period ended in 2002. Moreover, the interest rates emerging market countries had to pay on their debt came down as the risk of crises emanating from emerging markets diminished. Figure 15 plots the spread between the interest rates on sovereign debt in emerging market countries and the interest rates on U.S. Treasuries, showing how much risk levels declined in the period after the eight-year crisis. Although global financial crises flared up in 2007, the eight-year emerging market crisis period had come to an end.

Why did the crisis period end? In my view, changes in economic policy, motivated in part by new economic ideas, played a big role; those changes took place both in individual policies in the emerging market countries and in international monetary policy conducted by the International Monetary Fund and its major shareholders.

One valuable recommendation that came out of the research on financial crises is that individual emerging market countries could take steps to prevent or at least significantly reduce the likelihood of such crises. Models of financial crises developed in the 1990s and the actual experiences of policy makers with crises during those years showed that currency mismatches—large stocks of debt denominated in foreign currencies—could convert a currency depreciation into a major debt crisis. The models also showed that overly expansionary monetary policies under an exchange-rate peg could lead to a sudden and sharp depreciation, when investors realized that reserves would be insufficient to maintain the increasingly overvalued exchange rate.

The policy implications of this research were clear: avoid

currency mismatches, get inflation down and keep it down, adopt a more flexible exchange-rate policy, keep the debt-to-GDP ratio sustainable, and accumulate more foreign reserves. Many emerging market countries have learned such lessons and thus moved toward these sensible policies. Certainly reserves are higher and inflation is lower than during the eight-year crisis period. And, just as predicted by the theory and hoped by the theorists, the number of crises in the emerging markets declined.

In addition, the contagion of the crises declined sharply, which itself reduced the likelihood of crises. To see this, compare the global contagion following the Russian financial crisis in 1998 with the complete absence of contagion following the Argentine crisis just three years later, in 2001. I believe that policy changes in the operation of the international financial system were largely responsible for this decline in contagion of emerging market crises.

The most important international monetary lesson learned from the crisis period was the IMF's need to change the way in which it responds to financial crises—especially to be more deliberative and predictable about when it would exceed normal lending limits and provide large-scale assistance. In my view, this lack of predictability was a factor in the contagion of crises. According to most economic theories of contagion, in which less-informed investors tend to follow more-informed investors, surprise changes in policy are more likely to cause contagion than predicted or anticipated changes in policy. The idea that anticipated policy changes have a smaller impact than unanticipated changes goes back to the early days of rational expectations modeling.

The lack of predictability was most evident in the case of

Russia, where the IMF increased support in July 1998 and then one month later, in August 1998, indicated that it would remove support, a surprise that gave rise to the global contagion at the time. The IMF also demonstrated a lack of predictability in its responses to other crises. The Asian countries still feel that the IMF was not as responsive to their crises as it was to Mexico. The initial refusal to provide additional funds to Uruguay in 2002, which, if not reversed, would have severely disrupted the payments system, is another example. This assessment is not meant to be critical of individuals at the IMF. Indeed, the lack of predictability was due to a lack of a clear framework about how the IMF should operate in such situations; it reflected considerable disagreement among the shareholders about the role of the IMF.

Fortunately, the shareholders of the IMF came into much closer agreement on this issue and soon thereafter the crisis period seemed to end. They asked that the IMF introduce a more predictable decision framework into its operations, which the IMF did. Called the *exceptional access framework* (EAF), it was put in place in early 2003. The EAF represented a significant change in policy for the IMF, and it reflected a change in position by the G7 countries, in particular by the United States. In an action plan in April 2002, the G7 said that "we are prepared to limit official sector lending to normal access levels except when circumstances justify an exception. . . . Limiting official sector lending and developing private sector lending are essential parts of our Action Plan." The EAF states what the exceptions are and lists a set of principles or rules that determine whether IMF support will be provided. The EAF's aim, again in the words of the G7, was to "to increase predictability and reduce uncertainty about official policy actions in the emerging markets."

One barrier to the IMF's adopting the EAF was the lack of a reliable framework in which countries could engage with their private-sector creditors if and when sovereign debt needed to be restructured. Without such a framework it would be difficult for the IMF to adhere to any limits or rules. The IMF and its shareholders could say they were adopting limits but, when the crisis occurred, would be expected to abandon those limits. To deal with this problem, a new mechanism was proposed for the bond contracts. This mechanism—called collective action clauses (CACs)—made it possible for bond holders to allow their sovereign debtors to restructure their debt if need be. Hence a feasible and understandable "plan B" would be available to countries, allowing the IMF to say no if its limits were exceeded.

After a year of intense discussions in the international community, Mexico issued bonds in New York with collective action clauses for the first time in February 2003. Many other countries then followed. Those clauses represent a great improvement in the process of restructuring debt. In fact they go hand-in-hand with the EAF: the EAF was acceptable to IMF shareholders, management, and staff because it provided a procedure (the CACs) countries could use to restructure their debt without large-scale borrowing from the IMF.

Mission Impossible III

The third example is much more recent and, in fact, is still ongoing. I first suggested it in June 2007, before the recent financial crisis flared up. I was motivated by the concern that, in a highly globalized economy, one central bank going off track could lead to other central banks going off track and thereby bring the world back to conditions before Missions Impossible

I and II were accomplished. So the mission I suggested was "to prevent the forces of globalization from reversing the missions already accomplished."

When thinking about monetary policy in a global setting, central banks often take into consideration the interest rates set by other central banks. If there is concern about exchange-rate fluctuations, then moving the interest rate too far or too rapidly away from prevailing international interest rates could cause the currency to appreciate or depreciate, something the central bank might want to avoid. Many central bankers, even those with flexible exchange-rate policies, watch the federal funds rate set by the Federal Reserve when making policy decisions. This, however, could result in a significant departure from what would otherwise be an optimal policy for each country. Unless offset by other factors, large foreign interest-rate reactions could lead to policy mistakes.

To judge the seriousness of that problem, I estimated some values for the response coefficients for the European Central Bank (ECB) for the period from 2000 to 2006. I measured inflation as the four-quarter rate of change in the harmonized index of consumer prices and the real GDP gap as the percentage deviation of real GDP from its trend. I first computed the deviation from a Taylor rule. I then estimated the response of the deviation to the federal funds rate. The estimated response coefficient on the federal funds rate was .21 and statistically significant with a standard error of .056. The plot of the actual and fitted values from this equation is shown in Figure 5 in Chapter 1. A good part, but not all, of the negative deviation (where the ECB policy rate is below the rule) is explained by the federal funds rate being lower than normal. These strong foreign interest-rate effects are not unusual and are found in estimates of policy rules at other central banks, including the Federal Reserve.

Given the policy decisions since August 2007 as discussed in Chapters 2 and 3, Mission Impossible III is broader and more difficult than I originally conceived it two years ago. It is now more than keeping other countries from pushing each other off track, it is getting everyone back on track.: "Your mission, should you choose to accept it, is to get policy back on track and prevent the forces of globalization from reversing the missions already accomplished."

5

Why a Black Swan Landed in the Money Market in August 2007

The Fed has gone about as if the problem is a shortage of liquidity. That is not the basic problem. The basic problem for the markets is that uncertainty that the balance sheets of financial firms are credible.
—Anna J. Schwartz interviewed in the Wall Street Journal, October 18–19, 2008.

THE FAILURE TO DIAGNOSE the financial crisis early on as mainly due to increased risk rather than to liquidity is a key reason that the policy responses were inappropriate and that the crisis was prolonged, as explained in Chapter 2. As with a medical patient, say with cancer, if you misdiagnose the disease and see it as a digestive disorder, then you will prescribe the wrong treatment. By not attacking or removing the cancer you let it grow, and the treatment for a nonexistent digestive disorder could make the patient even sicker. Ironically, during the Great Depression, a crisis to which the current one is often compared, there was a liquidity shortage, and the Fed did not provide liquidity, as Milton Friedman and Anna Schwartz showed in their *Monetary History of the United States*. In this crisis the Fed did provide liquidity, but the problem was not a shortage of liquidity—the doctor prescribed the wrong treatment.

A legitimate and important question, however, is whether such a diagnosis was possible early on. In this chapter I examine this question. I explain how one goes about making such a diagnosis in the case of economic illnesses, and I examine some actual diagnoses made in real time in 2007 and 2008, including the one by John Williams and me mentioned in Chapter 2.

Early Signs

Signs of severe trouble first flared up on Thursday, August 9, 2007, when traders in New York, London, and other financial centers around the world faced a dramatic and sudden change in conditions in the money markets. Interest rates on medium-term interbank loans, measured, for example, by the three-month Libor (London Interbank Offered Rate) surged, compared with the interest rate on overnight interbank loans (the federal funds rate), which the Fed targets. The turmoil did not disappear. The term interbank rates did not come down at all and indeed moved up further on Friday. Rates on such term lending seemed to disconnect from the overnight rate and thereby from the Fed's target for interest rates. Because interest rates on trillions of dollars of loans and securities are linked to Libor, bringing the spread down became a major concern of policy officials at the Federal Reserve.

After many years of comparative calm, traders, bankers, and central bankers found these developments surprising and puzzling. But that Thursday and Friday of August 2007 turned out to be just the beginning of a remarkably long period of tumult in the money markets, with the difference between the three-month Libor and overnight loans remaining unusually high and volatile, reminiscent of the highly extraordinary events described by Nassim Taleb in his popular book *The Black Swan: The Impact of the Highly Improbable*. But why did that black swan land in the money markets?

Possible Diagnoses

Right from the beginning of the crisis, bankers, economists, and others offered various explanations. One explanation, referred to as "counterparty risk," was that banks became reluctant to lend to other banks because of the perception that the risk of default on the loans had increased and/or the market price of taking on such risk had risen. Lending between banks in the Libor interbank market is unsecured; there is no collateral to claim in the case of a default. Many banks were writing down their loans and securities because they had either been downgraded or were backed by mortgages with delinquent payments or foreclosed properties. Clearly, the continuing decline in housing prices and the slowing economy raised the chances of a further deterioration of banks' balance sheets. Moreover, the realization of the risks of securities backed by subprime mortgages triggered doubts about securities backed by all mortgages as well as other types of debt.

The other main explanation was an increased demand for, or shortage of, "liquidity." Indeed, liquidity was one of the most common explanations offered by market participants in interviews that I conducted early in the crisis; many at the time thought that liquidity was a more serious problem than counterparty risk. Liquidity is not always defined the same way by different market participants, and indeed the concept is elusive. Traders complain of a shortage of liquidity when their institutions do not allocate as much "balance sheet" to them to invest as they see the need for. In general, then, a liquidity problem involves a shortage of funds to lend.

To complicate things, however, there is also the related liquidity concept of "liquidity risk," which means that traders at one bank are reluctant to expose their bank's funds at a time when those funds might be needed to cover their own bank's shortfalls. In other words, risk associated with the lender's own balance sheet can appear to be a liquidity problem; in this case, however, balance sheet risk is the underlying factor rather than a pure shortage of liquidity.

A third explanation often heard during November 2007 through January 2008 was that banks were reluctant to lend to other banks because they wanted to be in safe liquid assets to make sure that their own balance sheets looked respectable in end-of-year financial reports, especially given the stress and scrutiny that many banks were under. As 2007 drifted into the past and the Libor remained higher than normal during the spring and summer of 2008, however, this explanation was given less credence, though it clearly could explain some movements in interest rates during part of the crisis.

A Diagnostic Tool: The Libor-OIS Spread

To distinguish between these explanations and diagnose the problem, a popular analytic approach called the *no-arbitrage* framework can be used. This is the framework I used with John Williams in the work we began in the fall of 2007. It is based on the idea that competitive forces drive differences between the yields on different securities to zero after adjusting for differences in maturity and risk. According to this framework, Libor at a certain maturity is a function of (1) *the average of expected future overnight interest rates* over the same maturity and (2) *risk factors* over the same maturity. To measure the average of expected overnight interest rates, a financial instrument called an overnight index swap (OIS) can be used.

An OIS has a certain maturity, such as three months, and works as follows: When the OIS matures, the parties exchange the difference between the interest that would be accrued from repeatedly rolling over an investment in the overnight market and the interest that would be accrued at the agreed OIS fixed rate. In contrast to Libor loans, OIS transactions involve little counterparty risk, as no money changes hands until the maturity date. The only potential loss in the case of default by the counterparty is the difference between the two interest rates on which the OIS is based. Thus, the OIS rate equals the average of the overnight interest rates expected until maturity. By subtracting the OIS rate from Libor, one removes this expectations effect. The difference between Libor and OIS, or the Libor-OIS spread, then becomes the focus of the diagnosis. Indeed, this is why the Libor-OIS spread was used extensively in Chapters 2 and 3;

Figure 7 in Chapter 2 shows how the Libor-OIS spread jumped on August 9, 2007.

From December 2001 (OIS data were not available before then) through August 8, 2007, the spread averaged 11 basis points with a standard deviation of about 4 basis points. It then rose sharply on August 9 and on subsequent days, eventually peaking at more than 100 basis points in early December 2007. This was followed by big downward movements in mid December 2007 and in mid January 2008, but the spread rose again in March 2008 and remained elevated until jumping even higher in September and October 2008. Looking at spreads going back to December 2001 illustrates just how unusual this episode has been. The spread averaged about 67 basis points from August 9, 2007, to August 8, 2008, about seventeen times the 4-basis-point standard deviation before the crisis—a 17-sigma event. And the spread was even wider in the fall of 2008.

Taking out these expectations from Libor using the OIS is essential to understanding whether risk or liquidity changes the spreads. Expectations of declining overnight rates, for example, will cause term Libor to decline, all else equal. Hence for the first part of the crisis period, expectations effects tended to reduce the spread between Libor and the target Fed funds rate because of expectations of future interest-rate declines due to policy easing. Indeed, in mid February 2008, the spread narrowed significantly, probably due to expectations of larger future interest-rate cuts.

The Libor-OIS spread can also be used to examine conditions in other countries. Figure 16 shows the Libor-OIS spreads in euros and sterling along with the dollar Libor-OIS spread.

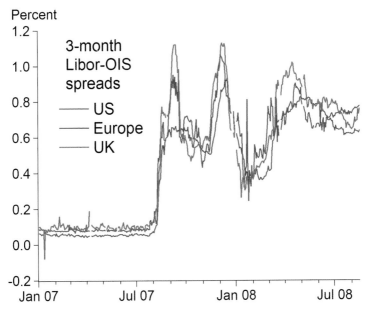

Figure 16. The Libor-OIS Spread in Three Major Currencies

Clearly the turmoil affecting money markets was not limited to dollar loans between banks in the United States: Libor-OIS spreads also rose on euro loans in the euro area and sterling loans in the United Kingdom. All three spreads move closely together. This close correspondence in spreads is not as surprising as it first may appear because there is considerable overlap in banks that are included in the Libor survey in the three countries. Table 2 lists the banks participating in the Libor survey; the U.S., European, and United Kingdom lists include fourteen of the same banks (out of sixteen in each survey).

Table 2. Banks in the Libor Survey

United States	Europe	United Kingdom
Bank of America	Bank of America	Bank of America
Bank of Tokyo–Mitsubishi UFJ	Bank of Tokyo–Mitsubishi UFJ	Bank of Tokyo–Mitsubishi UFJ
Barclays Bank	Barclays Bank	Barclays Bank
Citibank NA	Citibank NA	Citibank NA
Deutsche Bank	Deutsche Bank	Deutsche Bank
HBOS	HBOS	HBOS
HSBC	HSBC	HSBC
JP Morgan Chase	JP Morgan Chase	JP Morgan Chase
Lloyds TSB Bank	Lloyds TSB Bank	Lloyds TSB Bank
Rabobank	Rabobank	Rabobank
Royal Bank of Canada	Royal Bank of Canada	Royal Bank of Canada
Royal Bank of Scotland Group	Royal Bank of Scotland Group	Royal Bank of Scotland Group
UBS AG	UBS AG	UBS AG
West LB AG	West LB AG	West LB AG
Credit Suisse	Credit Suisse	Abbey National
Norinchukin Bank	Société Générale	BNP Paribas

Measures of Counterparty Risk and the Diagnosis

To determine empirically whether the increased Libor-OIS spread was due to counterparty risk, one needs a measure of counterparty risk. Because any single measure is an imperfect proxy, using multiple measures increases the robustness of the diagnosis. Fortunately there are a number of possible measures available. John Williams and I used three in our work. By examining how these measures correlate with the Libor-OIS spread, we could determine whether rising risks were the main reason for the increased spread in the interbank markets.

Credit Default Swaps. One potential measure of counterparty risk is the probability of banks defaulting on their debt. Those probabilities can be assessed using the premiums on a financial instrument called credit default swaps (CDS), which are essentially insurance policies on corporate bonds. The buyer of a credit default swap pays a periodic fee to a seller in exchange for the promise of a payment, in the event of bankruptcy or default, of the difference between the par value and the market value of the corporate bond.

CDS rates for banks participating in the U.S. dollar Libor survey rose in the summer of 2007. Hence, by this measure, counterparty risk looks like a good candidate for explaining the increase in Libor-OIS spreads, which also rose in the summer of 2007. A large spike in the CDS market occurred during the period of the Bear Stearns crisis in March 2008. Then, following JP Morgan's purchase of Bear Stearns, CDS rates fell but then rose again and remained high through the summer of 2008, reflecting investor concerns regarding the conditions of the major banks in the Libor survey.

The Libor-Tibor Spread. A second market-based measure of risk in the U.S. banking sector can be constructed by comparing Libor with interest rates on interbank loans for a group of banks that are less affected by the problems related to U.S. mortgage-related securities than the banks in the Libor survey. A natural candidate for such a measure is the interbank loan market in Japan where many non-U.S. and non-European banks, which had fewer problems with mortgage-backed securities on their balance sheets, participate. The Tokyo Inter-Bank Offered Rate (Tibor) is the interest rate on yen-denominated loans in the Japanese interbank market. It is computed from the same kind of survey used to compute Libor except that the banks are mainly Japanese. There is also a yen-denominated Libor survey in which most of the participants are the same banks as in the dollar-denominated Libor survey.

The spread between Libor denominated in yen and Tibor denominated in yen thus provides an independent measure of counterparty risk for the banks in the U.S.-dollar Libor survey, relative to that of the banks in the Tibor survey. In the late 1990s, Japanese banks experienced sizable spreads on interbank loans. Risks in the banking sector in Tokyo caused interest rates on interbank loans to rise in Tokyo compared with London. In other words, Tibor rates rose relative to Libor rates.

That pattern of Libor-Tibor spreads reversed during the present crisis, with Tibor rates now lower than corresponding Libor rates. The most likely explanation is that the risks associated with interbank loans from U.S. and European banks have increased relative to those for loans among Japanese banks. Thus the Libor-Tibor spread is another measure of counterparty risk among banks in New York, London, and Frankfurt that also shows movement at the same time as the Libor-OIS spread. To be sure, one could argue that the demand for liquidity rose as much for Japanese banks as for the major banks in those other markets, but, given anecdotal and other information that the balance sheets deteriorated more in the other countries than in Japan, differences in risk factors are more plausible.

Libor-Repo Spreads. A third market-based measure of risk is the spread between interest rates on unsecured and secured lending in the interbank market. The greater the risk of non-payment of the loan, the higher the spread should be, all else equal. Repurchase agreements (repos) between banks backed by Treasury securities are a form of secured lending. In contrast, Libor measures the interest rate on unsecured loans. Hence the spread between Libor and repo rates of the same maturity is effectively the spread between unsecured and secured loans, a natural measure of counterparty risk. This measure is also closely tied to the Libor-OIS spread, as shown in Figure 8 in Chapter 2. Although there is more noise in this spread than in the Libor-OIS spread, it clearly turns up about the same time as the Libor-OIS spread. Traders attribute the noise to technical factors, such as tax considerations and collateral delivery glitches.

In sum, all three independent measures of counterparty risk are closely correlated with the Libor-OIS spread. Indeed, as Figure 8 makes clear, there is not much room for any other factor. Given these results, the diagnosis that the problems in the money market, as represented by the heightened Libor-OIS spread, were mainly due to anything but risk would be questionable.

The Term Auction Facility

Nevertheless, in December 2007 the Federal Reserve created a term auction facility (TAF) aimed specifically at providing liquidity directly to financial institutions to improve the functioning of the money markets and drive down the Libor-OIS spread. As stated by the Federal Reserve Board at the time the TAF was created, by injecting "term funds through a broader range of counterparties and against a broader range of collateral than open market operations, this facility could help ensure that liquidity provisions can be disseminated efficiently even when the unsecured interbank markets are under stress."

The TAF allows financial institutions to make bids for term borrowing from the Fed, originally for a maturity of twenty-eight days. Beginning in late December 2007, two TAF auctions were held each month. TAF loans are collateralized with the Fed setting the auction amount. It set the minimum bid equal to the OIS rate corresponding to the term of the loan. At the same time that the TAF was introduced, other central banks, including the Bank of Canada, the Bank of England, the European Central Bank (ECB), and the Swiss National Bank (SNB), also took measures to increase term lending. The ECB and SNB launched their own term auction facilities beginning in December 2007. The total volume of outstanding TAF loans, including those from the Federal Reserve, ECB, and SNB, is shown in Figure 9 in Chapter 2, along with the amount from the Federal Reserve TAF auctions alone. The ECB's and SNB's TAF auctions were halted for a while early in 2008 before beginning again with larger auction amounts in March 2008.

Early reports on the effectiveness of the TAF were generally favorable. All the early TAF auctions were oversubscribed, and the TAF auction rate was generally well above the prevailing one-month OIS rate, indicating substantial demand for TAF borrowing. Moreover, as noted above, Libor-OIS spreads fell sharply between late December 2007 and February 2008. As a result, central bank officials and others judged that the TAF was working. For example, in mid February 2008, Frederic Mishkin, then a governor of the Federal Reserve Board, noted the decline in the term spread, stating that "the TAF may have had significant beneficial effects on financial markets. . . . term funding rates have dropped substantially relative to OIS rates: The one-month spread exceeded 100 basis points in early December but has dropped below 30 basis points in recent weeks—though still above the low level that prevailed before the onset of the financial disruption last August." During this period, people began to think that diagnoses that the problem was primarily risk, such as mine and John Williams's, were incorrect. The reduction in the spread was short lived, however, as a quick glance back at Figure 9 will show. As time went by and the spread continued to remain high, the idea that the TAF was reducing the spreads seemed less and less plausible. And because the TAF was designed to provide liquidity, its ineffectiveness in reducing Libor-OIS raised additional questions about the liquidity explanation of the financial stresses and confirmed the original diagnosis that the problem was risk.

Further Confirmation of the Risk Diagnosis

More formal statistical regression techniques further confirmed these results. In a regression, you estimate whether a dependent variable, such as the Libor-OIS spread, depends on independent variables, such as a counterparty risk measure and the TAF. The independent variables in this case are CDS rates, the Libor-Tibor spreads, and the Libor-repo spreads, as well as measures of the TAF. The TAF can be measured in various ways using a TAF indicator or "dummy" variable. For example one indicator dummy could be set to one on the day of the TAF auction and zero at other times. Another indicator could be set to one for the day of a TAF auction and several days following.

In John Williams's and my regression analysis, the risk measures entered with the correct sign and were usually highly significant. The results were robust across different measures of the dependent variable and the different measure of counterparty risk. For example, in a typical equation a 1 percentage point increase in the median CDS rate was associated with between a 0.56 and 0.69 percentage point increase in spreads. In contrast, the impacts of the TAF indicators were not robust or significant. The signs of the TAF impacts were in some cases positive and in others negative. In no case were the TAF variables both negative and statistically significant.

After John Williams and I wrote our initial working paper on this subject, others reported similar tests, focusing on the Libor-OIS spread with a variety of alternative specifications. By the fall of 2008 there was general agreement that counterparty risk is the main explanatory factor behind the increased Libor-OIS spread, although some economists in the Federal Reserve system found the TAF to have been more effective in reducing spreads. Tao Wu of the Dallas Federal Reserve Bank defined a TAF dummy that equals 0 before the TAF was first announced on December 12, 2007, and 1 since then. That specification is based on the hypothesis that introducing the TAF would permanently reduce spreads in the interbank lending markets. Wu found that such a TAF variable had a significant and negative effect. Those initial findings probably reflected the decline in spreads near the end of 2007 and in early 2008; they diminished as the spreads increased later in 2008, as I discussed in the context of Governor Mishkin's remarks. A group of researchers at the New York Fed, James McAndrews, Asani Sarkar, and Zhenyu Wang, took a different approach and found that the announcements and the operations of the TAF combined had a significant negative effect on changes in the spread. John Williams and I, however, found that their results were not robust using the alternative measures of risk.

In any case, by late 2008, after the crisis was more than a year old, most researchers were in agreement that counterparty risk was the primary driving factor. By this time more of the focus of government policy had been placed on the balance sheets of the banks. If that diagnosis had been accepted a year earlier, the actions to remove bad assets or inject equity into the banks could have begun much earlier.

Epilogue

IN THIS BOOK I have provided empirical evidence that government actions and interventions caused, prolonged, and worsened the financial crisis. They caused it by deviating from historical precedents and principles for setting interest rates that had worked well for twenty years. They prolonged it by misdiagnosing the problems in the bank credit markets and thereby responding inappropriately, focusing on liquidity rather than risk. They made it worse by supporting certain financial institutions and their creditors but not others in an ad hoc way, without a clear and understandable framework. Although other factors were certainly at play, those government actions should be first on the list of answers to the question of what went wrong.

I also provided evidence that it does not have to be this way. By systematically conducting policy according to a set of sound market principles with minimal deviations and interventions for two decades, policy makers delivered an outstanding performance called the Great Moderation. Similarly, by adopting such systematic policies internationally, they ended the severe eight-year emerging markets crisis period that began in the mid 1990s.

What are the implications of this analysis for the future? The first implication is that policy makers should rethink the idea that frequent and large government actions and interventions are the only answer to our current economic problems. Such a philosophy could take us further off track and, according to the analysis in this book, could make things worse rather than better. Since the research underlying this book was completed, however, strong indications are that this first recommendation will be difficult to achieve in practice. On December 16, 2008, George W. Bush said that "to make sure the economy doesn't collapse. I've abandoned free market principles to save the free market system." And on January 8, 2009, Barack Obama said, "Only government can break the vicious cycles that are crippling our economy."

The second implication is that it is important to lay the groundwork for getting on track again by reinstating or establishing a set of principles to follow to prevent misguided actions and interventions in the future. Although policy is now in a massive cleanup mode, getting on track must be part of the cleanup, including

- Returning to the set of principles for setting interest rates that worked well during the Great Moderation
- Basing any future government interventions on a clearly stated diagnosis of the problem and a rationale for the interventions

- Creating a predictable exceptional access framework for providing financial assistance to existing financial institutions—the IMF's exceptional access framework that guides its lending decisions to emerging market countries is a good example to follow.

Some of these reforms require rethinking the international financial architecture; others are purely domestic. For example, to keep policy interest rates on track in a globalized economy, it would help to introduce the notion of a global inflation target [3], which would help prevent rapid cuts in interest rates in one country if they perversely affected decisions in other countries. Policy makers could then discuss global goals for inflation and the impact that one central bank might have on such inflation. In contrast, developing exceptional access frameworks for central banks and finance ministries could be done in each country without a global structure. Similarly, setting controls on leveraging at the financial institutions could also be done in each country.

Finally, I want to stress that the part of the research presented in this book that is on the current crisis must be considered preliminary. We are still in the middle of the crisis, and more data need to be collected and analyzed. There are and will continue to be differences of opinion. Carefully documented empirical research is needed to sort out those differences. We should base our policy evaluations and conclusions on empirical analyses, not on ideological, personal, political, or partisan grounds.

Frequently Asked Questions

THE FOLLOWING QUESTIONS are representative of those that people have asked about the material in this book. They have been compiled from radio and TV interviews, blogs, conferences, e-mails, and meetings with students and colleagues.

What is a counterfactual? This is a method that economic historians use to analyze cause and effect. If you want to estimate the effect of an economic policy or event, consider what would have happened if that policy or event had not occurred by hypothesizing what might have happened instead. A famous example in economic history concerns the debate about the importance of the railroads in U.S. economic growth; the counterfactual is that, without railroads, people would have had to use roads, rivers, and canals instead. The historian then must figure out how different westward expansion or the development of new products would have been if people had had to rely on only those means of transportation.

In this book I use the counterfactual approach to investigate what would have happened had the Fed not held interest rates as low as it did in the period from 2002 to 2004. To answer the question of what would have happened if the Fed followed the Taylor rule (the counterfactual), I used a model of the effects of a different interest rate on housing. Counterfactuals are used elsewhere in this book but less formally. For example, to address the question about the impact of misdiagnosing the cause of the black swan in the money market, one might assume that the government had not introduced the TAF in December 2007 but had instead begun providing capital to banks or buying their toxic assets in December 2007. I assume that this counterfactual would have resulted in a shorter, less severe crisis, though we do not have a formal economic model.

More generally this book contends that, in the counterfactual event that policy did not "get off track," then we would have had a continuation of the Great Moderation.

What is the Great Moderation? First noticed by economists in the mid 1990s, this refers to the period from the early 1980s to around 2007, when the U.S. economy was much more stable than in other periods. Not only were inflation and interest rates and their volatilities diminished, compared with the experience of the 1970s, but the volatility of real GDP had reached lows never seen before. Economic expansions had become longer and stronger, and recessions had become rarer and shorter. I called this phenomenon the Long Boom because it was as if there was one long growth expansion, beginning with the end of the deep recession in 1982 and continuing right through its fifteenth anniversary in 1997, with the mild 1990–91 recession seeming like a small interruption compared to recessions of the past. Others called the phenomenon the Great Moderation because of the general decline in volatility of output growth and the inflation rate.

The Great Moderation or the Long Boom lurks behind the scenes in this study because its stable macroeconomic behavior is in such contrast to the financial crisis and serious recession that began in 2007.

What is the Taylor rule? The Taylor rule is a recommendation of how the Fed or any other central bank should set the short-term interest rate. It says that the Fed should raise the interest rate when inflation increases and lower it when GDP declines, as in a recession. More important, it says by *how much* the interest rate should change in those circumstances. To be precise, the Taylor rule says that the interest rate should be one-and-a-half times the inflation rate plus one-half times the GDP gap plus one. (The GDP gap measures how far GDP is from its normal trend level.) So, in 1989, for example, when the federal funds rate was about 10 percent in the United States, one could say that the 10 percent was equal to 1.5 times the inflation rate of 5 percent (or 7.5) plus 0.5 times the GDP gap of about 3 percent (or 1.5, which takes you to 9) plus 1, which gives you 10. This very specific rule can be written down with algebra, as I did when I first wrote it down in 1992. Of course, I didn't call it the Taylor rule; others did that later.

Isn't the Taylor rule simply a description of what central banks do rather than a recommendation of what they should do? The rule was originally meant to be a recommendation of what the Fed should do to keep inflation low and recessions mild and infrequent; in other words, it was meant to be normative rather than positive. It was derived from monetary theory or more precisely, from monetary models that describe how the interest rate affects the economy. Like most rules or laws in economics, it is not as precise as most physical laws, though that does not mean it is less useful. It was certainly not meant to be used mechanically but rather as a guide embodying important principles.

Over time, however, people began to observe that the policy rule was often accurate at predicting future interest rates. As John Judd and Bharat Trehan of the San Francisco Fed said in a 1995 paper: "Taylor had already shown that his rule closely fit the actual path of the funds rate from 1987 (when Alan Greenspan became Fed Chairman) to 1992 (when Taylor did his study). [We show] that the same close relationship continued to hold over 1993 and 1994 as well." This was probably the most amazing thing to observers at the time because nobody had any idea that this was going to happen back in 1992. If they try, economists can always fit equations to past data, but rarely do things come out so well in the future, after the work is done.

The rule was not designed for forecasting; it was meant to be normative, not positive, yet it turned out to be both. This predictive value obviously interested business economists and policy makers, especially those working in the financial markets. John Lipsky, then at Salomon Brothers, and Gavyn Davies at Goldman Sachs, for example, wrote newsletters as early as 1995 and 1996 that used monetary rules to forecast and analyze Fed decisions. Janet Yellen, then a member of the Board of Governors of the Federal Reserve, referred to monetary policy rules in a speech at a meeting of the National Association for Business Economics in March 1996, mentioning their predictive power.

Are there alternative policy rules? There are many others. Milton Friedman's constant-growth-rate rule said hold money growth constant and let the interest rate go where it might. Bennett McCallum of Carnegie Mellon University proposed a flexible rule for the monetary base. In contrast, the Taylor rule is about the interest rate rather than the money supply. Other monetary policy rules for setting the interest rate include those that look at forecasts of inflation and real GDP rather than their current values; others gradually adjust the federal funds rate. Still others react to the price level rather than to the inflation rate. But they are all similar in that they describe the settings for the interest rate and embody the key principles.

There has been a great debate over the years about the use of monetary policy rules; they were not always pervasive, and there was a great deal of resistance to them at central banks until the 1980s. Since then thousands of articles and papers have been written on the Taylor and other policy rules. The staffs of the Fed and other central banks use those policy rules for analysis, including scenarios of what might happen when they go off the rules. Policy rules became important in central banking circles because of the need for a framework in which to make decisions about policy. In addition, there is a firm basis for the use of policy rules in modern economics thanks to the research of economists such as the Nobel prize winners Robert Lucas of the University of Chicago and Edward Prescott of Arizona State University.

What is your response to former Federal Reserve Board chairman Alan Greenspan's criticism of the counterfactual presented in Chapter 1? He wrote in the *Financial Times* Economists Forum on April 6, 2008: "Taylor (with whom I rarely disagree) and others derive their simulations from model structures that

have been consistently unable to anticipate the onset of recessions or financial crises. This suggests important missing variables. Counterfactuals from such flawed structures cannot form the basis for policy." The model used for the counterfactual in Chapter 1 was designed to show the empirical relation between the federal funds rate and housing starts. It was not meant to forecast recessions or financial crises but rather to show how deviations of the interest rate from a policy rule could lead to a housing boom. No model is perfect, but I always say you need an alternative model to criticize a model, and I have not seen one that delivers conclusions different from mine. Using a completely different model, European Central Bank economists Marek Jarocinski and Frank Smets came to the same conclusion as I did. Hence, I do not think that the criticism applies.

Is it tough to write a book critical of the policy decisions of people you know well and have worked with for many years? Yes, of course. It was tough when I stood up and first presented the material in Chapter 1 to more than one hundred central bankers and financial analysts from all over the world at the Jackson Hole conference in the summer of 2007—people whom I respect and whom I count as friends. I had been going to that conference for many of the past twenty-five years and never written such a critical analysis of policy. But overall the reaction has been positive. Some central bankers quietly say they agree with me. Others thank me for doing it, one saying, for example, "your courage in putting forth your criticisms directly is admirable." Others disagree but appreciate my taking an as objective as possible look at the data and getting away from personalities and partisanship and politics. In my view economists and other professionals outside government, in civil society, have an obligation to speak out when their research shows a policy to be ineffective or to cause harm, even when their friends are responsible for the policy. Milton Friedman, who used to write a column in *Newsweek*, heavily criticized Arthur Burns when he was Chairman of the Fed in the 1970s in many of those columns, even though Burns was his friend and former economics teacher who first got him interested in economics.

You emphasize that the empirical results are still preliminary. When will we figure out for sure what really went wrong? Is it something we'll reach consensus about two years from now or twenty or thirty years from now? We will be debating about what went wrong for many years. That's what happened after the Great Depression of the 1930s. Not until the 1960s did Milton Friedman and Anna Schwartz complete their definitive monetary study of the period. And only then did a consensus develop among economists that the Great Depression was in large part due to monetary phenomena and in particular to the Federal Reserve letting money growth decline. In writing this book now, my purpose is to learn whatever lessons we can and move forward. Like all analyses written close in time to actual events, this book has the advantage of conveying lessons while they are fresh and can be applied immediately. Obviously there's more work to be done, but we already have a pile of data and radically improved information technology, so why wait thirty years? In my view the basic thesis of this book—that government policies caused, prolonged, and worsened the crisis—will survive further scrutiny, though the exact details and reasons will evolve as more information is accumulated.

If there were monetary excesses in the years around 2002 to 2005, why didn't we see inflation rise? The inflation rate was rising. Using the consumer price index, the inflation rate was 1.6 percent in 2002, 2.3 percent in 2003, 2.7 percent in 2004, 3.4 percent in 2005, and 3.3 percent in 2006. Most people had assumed that the implicit goal for inflation at the Fed was around 2 percent, yet it was above that rate and rising through the period. But I think you have to look at more than inflation to assess the situation. Monetary economists have been concerned for years about the erratic nature of monetary policy, creating booms and then slamming on the brakes. Milton Friedman's *Newsweek* columns were filled with that kind of complaint. In my view that has been a major problem with monetary policy in the past few years, after two decades of good systematic performance beginning in the early 1980s.

Although your analysis focuses on the government policy responses, didn't major blunders occur in the private sector as well? Just as the Federal Reserve abandoned the Taylor rule, didn't the senior managers of the large financial institutions abandon well-tested risk management principles? Yes. Leverage ratios got too high, and there was too little diversification away from the risk that depended on housing prices. But the search for those higher yields was partially due to a low interest-rate policy. In addition, existing regulatory and supervisory oversight rules were not enforced properly by the Federal Reserve or the Securities and Exchange Commission. Government actions and interventions should be at the top of the list of causes, not the only causes. Perhaps one silver lining from this episode is that it has exposed these management and regulatory blunders, as well as the truly fraudulent schemes made famous by Madoff and others.

Although it was counterparty risk that drove the Libor-OIS spreads upward, wasn't the problem at least partly due to liquidity risk? As usually defined, liquidity risk is a problem when financial institutions reduce their willingness to lend long term because they are not sure about the quality of their own assets or are worried about depositor withdrawals or client redemptions. John Williams and I tried to test for this by comparing rates on bank-to-bank lending versus everybody-else-to-bank lending. Accordingly, we compared Libor and interest rates on certificates of deposit (CD), which are held by individuals and nonbanks. We found that the interest rate on CDs followed Libor closely during the period of the crisis. As long as lenders exist who are not constrained by liquidity concerns, banks who seek to hoard liquidity can borrow from these lenders in the CD market. Large CDs with a term of one year or less are a major source of bank deposits. That CD rates tracked Libor closely during the crisis suggests that liquidity concerns at banks are not a significant factor separate from counterparty risk driving term lending rates. One problem with this test is that some lenders in the CD market might have the same liquidity risk problems as banks were purported to have.

Among government agencies, isn't too much blame placed on the Federal Reserve? This book also raises questions about fiscal policy decisions (the temporary rebates), implementation of policy by the administration (such as the lack of clarity in the operation of the TARP), and regulatory policy (the failure to rein in Fannie and Freddie). The last of these is an example of government regulatory failure. So it is certainly not only the Federal Reserve.

Why does Figure 11 on oil prices not show the fall in oil prices after the summer and fall of 2008? The fall in oil prices in the period beyond the data plotted in Figure 11 was likely due to the sharp decline in the world economy and the deteriorating economic outlook. It is difficult to show these forces in a diagram, but they can be taken into account using models estimated with regression techniques, such as the ones used at the International Monetary Fund, referred to in Chapter 2.

Wasn't the problem with the Federal Reserve policy in 2002–5 that rates were not raised fast enough rather than that they were taken too low? If the counterfactual is that the Fed took rates down to 1 percent but raised them more slowly than in Figure 1, then the impact on housing starts is similar to that in Figure 2. In other words there still would have been a boom and a bust. So I think the results are robust to such an alternative counterfactual.

Wasn't it reasonable for the Fed to cut interest rates in late 2007 and early 2008? Yes. With output declining it was correct to cut rates in the first six months of the crisis. The problem was that the federal funds rate came down too rapidly during that period which is why I used it as an example in Chapter 2.

Don't you run the risk of falsely attributing causation to correlation, especially with the advantage of having information that the people making decisions did not have? There is certainly such a risk. The passage of time and more information about how the policy decisions were made will help sort out cause and effect. Using explicit counterfactuals with models, as I have tried to do where possible, helps prevent this. Also much of the research work underlying this book was done in real time without the advantage of hindsight.

Doesn't housing demand depend mainly on long-term interest rates that were not affected much by monetary policy during this period? Housing demand also depends on short rates because of adjustable rate mortgages, which were about one-third of the mortgage market during the height of the boom. Moreover, the failure of long-term rates to adjust to monetary policy during this period was in part due to the decision to hold short rates down for too long, which likely affected expectations of future short rates and thereby long-term interest rates. In other words when bond investors and traders observed the small or negligible movement of the short-term rate, they might have felt that the Fed had departed from the kind of rule that formed the basis of the larger long-term interest-rate responses in earlier years.

What is your response to Federal Reserve Board vice chairman Donald Kohn, who argued in his October 2007 speech, "John Taylor Rules," that actual and core CPI inflation measures diverged substantially between 2003 and 2005 and that core measures would bring the Taylor rule prescriptions much closer to the actual path of policy than that shown in Figure 1? The Taylor rule was not formulated with core inflation; to avoid overreacting to short-term fluctuations in inflation, I recommended taking the average inflation rate over four quarters. Guiding policy by core inflation would make sense for short-term divergences between core and actual, but for three or more consecutive years of divergences, it is questionable. In that speech Don Kohn raised several other questions about using a policy rule during that period, including uncertainty about measuring potential GDP, widening credit spreads, and risk management issues, including the risk of a Japan-style deflation. Those considerations point out the real difficulties of making decisions in real time and why evaluating policy decisions with the benefit of hindsight should be done with caution. But overall I think the lesson learned from this period is that interest rates were too low.

I greatly appreciate Don Kohn and others for taking the time to give different perspectives on these important issues. In my view, having a thorough discussion is essential to getting back on track.

Milton Friedman is often quoted as saying, "The Great Depression, like most other periods of severe unemployment, was produced by government mismanagement rather than by any inherent instability of the private economy." Does that statement apply to the current financial crisis and period of severe unemployment? Yes.

References

THE EMPIRICAL RESEARCH PROJECTS on which this book is built are summarized below. Further details about the methods, results, terminology, and relation to work by other researchers are found in these references. All the references are available on the Global Markets Working Group website at the Hoover Institution: www.hoover.org/research/globalmarkets

1. "Housing and Monetary Policy," in *Housing, Housing Finance, and Monetary Policy* (Kansas City: Federal Reserve Bank of Kansas City, 2007). This paper reported on research completed in the summer of 2007, before the August flare-up in the financial markets. It focuses on the relationship between monetary policy and the housing boom. It was delivered as a speech at a policy panel at the annual Jackson Hole conference, August 30–September 1, 2007.

2. "Globalization and Monetary Policy: Missions Impossible," in Mark Gertler and Jordi Gali, eds., *The International Dimensions*

of Monetary Policy (University of Chicago Press for National Bureau of Economic Research, 2009). This paper summarizes research on globalization and monetary policy, aimed at the potential problem caused by central banks following each other, either directly or indirectly, explaining why several central banks held interest rates too low in 2002–4, as discussed in Chapter 1. The paper was delivered as a speech at an NBER conference in Girona, Spain, on June 11, 2007. A condensed and adapted version of this paper is found in Chapter 4.

3. "A Black Swan in the Money Market," with John C. Williams. This research project on the reasons for the turmoil in the money markets began in the fall of 2007, with a focus on determining whether risk or liquidity was responsible for the unusual jump in interbank lending rates in August 2007. A working paper (no. 2008-04) with the same title was issued by the Federal Reserve Bank of San Francisco in April and another working paper, "Further Results on a Black Swan in the Money Market," was issued in May by the Stanford Institute for Economic Policy Research. The final version was published in the *American Economic Journal: Macroeconomics*, 1, no.1 (2009): 58–83. Chapter 5 is largely based on this paper.

4. "The State of the Economy and Principles for Fiscal Stimulus," testimony before the Senate Budget Committee, November 19, 2008. The testimony reported on a project to estimate the impact of the tax rebates of 2008 on the economy. More formal econometric evidence was presented in a paper prepared for the American Economic Association meeting in San Francisco in January 2009 and published with the title "The Lack of an Empirical Rationale for the Revival of Discretionary Fiscal Policy," *American Economic Review, Papers and Proceedings*, May 2009.

5. "The Costs and Benefits of Deviating from the Systematic Component of Monetary Policy," keynote address at the Federal Reserve Bank of San Francisco conference on "Monetary Policy

and Asset Markets," February 22, 2008; "Monetary Policy and the State of the Economy," testimony before the House Financial Services Committee, February 26, 2008. This research examined whether monetary policy rules should be adjusted for the increased spread in the money markets.

6. "The Way Back to Stability and Growth in the Global Economy," *Monetary and Economic Studies*, 26 (December 2008): 37–47, was presented as the inaugural Mayekawa Lecture at the Bank of Japan in May 2008. It discusses the impact of the sharp monetary easing on oil and other commodity prices and proposes a global inflation target as a means of preventing central banks' interest-rate decisions from spreading to other central banks.

7. "Toward a New Framework for Exceptional Access" was a presentation at the conference on "The Future Role of Central Banking Policy: Urgent and Precedent-Setting Next Steps," held at Stanford University on July 22, 2008. The presentation laid out the case for developing a more systematic approach to the Fed's interventions and bailouts of financial institutions or their creditors. It followed the Bear Stearns intervention but preceded the Lehman bankruptcy.

Acknowledgments

I AM GRATEFUL to many people for help and comments on the research papers underlying this book or the book itself, including Annelise Anderson, Martin Anderson, Marshall Blanchard, John Cogan, Darrell Duffie, Alan Greenspan, Stephen Langlois, Angelo Melino, John Murray, Jennifer Navarrette, James Poterba, Jennifer Presley, John Seater, Eugene Shanks, Alvin Rabushka, John Raisian, Peter Robinson, George Shultz, Marie-Christine Slakey, Josie Smith, Johannes Stroebel, Allyn Taylor, Daniel Thornton, and Ann Wood.

Much of this material was originally presented at the Global Markets Working Group at the Hoover Institution at Stanford University, and I thank all the participants in that group for that opportunity and for their feedback. I especially thank John Williams for our collaborations on the black swan research. I am also grateful to the Hoover Institution for research support.

The chapters in this book are based on research papers that have been published elsewhere. Chapters 1 through 3 are based on the paper "The Financial Crisis and the Policy Responses: An Empirical Analysis of What Went Wrong," in the *David Dodge Festschrift*, Bank of Canada, 2009. Chapter 4 was adapted from the paper, "Globalization and Monetary Policy: Missions Impossible," in Jordi Gali and Mark Gertler, eds, *The International Dimensions of Monetary Policy* (National Bureau of Economic Research, University of Chicago Press, 2009). Chapter 5 was adapted from "A Black Swan in the Money Market," with John C. Williams, *American Economic Journal Macroeconomics*, 1, no. 1. (January 2009): 58–83. I am grateful to the Bank of Canada, the National Bureau of Economic Research, the University of Chicago Press, and the American Economic Association for permission to use published material.

About the Author

JOHN B. TAYLOR is the Bowen H. and Janice Arthur McCoy Senior Fellow at the Hoover Institution and the Mary and Robert Raymond Professor of Economics at Stanford University. He has served as the director of the Stanford Institute for Economic Policy Research (SIEPR) and was founding director of Stanford's Introductory Economics Center.

Taylor's fields of expertise are monetary and international economics. In the 1970s and 1980s he was a pioneer in developing new empirical procedures to evaluate monetary policy; in the early 1990s he formalized this work in the Taylor Rule for conducting monetary policy. Many economists think that adherence of central banks to the principles underlying this rule was a major reason for two decades of extraordinarily stable economic performance.

He has also participated in public policy. He served as senior economist on President Ford's and President Carter's Council of Economic Advisers in 1976 and 1977 and as a member of President George H.W. Bush's Council of Economic Advisers from 1989 through 1991. He was a member of the Congressional Budget Office's Panel of Economic Advisers from 1995 to 2001 and a senior economic adviser to the Bob Dole presidential campaign in 1996, the George W. Bush presidential campaign in 2000, and the John McCain campaign in 2008. He is currently a member of Governor Schwarzenegger's Council of Economic Advisers.

For four years, from 2001 to 2005, Taylor served as undersecretary of the Treasury for international affairs, where he was responsible for U.S. policies in international finance, including currency markets, trade in financial services, foreign investment, international debt, and oversight of the International Monetary Fund and the World Bank. He was also responsible for coordinating financial policy with the G-7 countries and was a member of the Board of the Overseas Private Investment Corporation. His book *Global Financial Warriors: The Untold Story of International Finance in the Post 9/11 World* gives a behind-the-scenes look at international economic policy making.

Taylor was awarded the Alexander Hamilton Award for his leadership in international finance at the U.S. Treasury, the Treasury Distinguished Service Award for designing and implementing the currency reforms in Iraq, and the Medal of the Republic of Uruguay for his work in resolving the 2002 financial crisis. In 2006 SIEPR awarded Taylor the George P. Shultz Distinguished Public Service Award, and in 2007 the National Association for Business Economics awarded him the Adam Smith Award for his work as a groundbreaking researcher, public servant, and teacher during a career of more than thirty years and his outstanding leadership in the field of economics.

Taylor has also won several teaching awards, including the Hoagland Prize for excellence in undergraduate teaching and the Rhodes Prize for his high ratings in teaching Stanford's introductory economics course. He also received a Guggenheim Fellowship for his research. He is a fellow of the American Academy of Arts and Sciences and the Econometric Society and formerly served as vice president of the American Economic Association.

Before joining the Stanford faculty in 1984, Taylor held positions as professor of economics at Princeton University and Columbia University. Taylor received a B.A. in economics summa cum laude from Princeton University in 1968 and a Ph.D. in economics from Stanford University in 1973.

Index

Other Books by John B. Taylor

GLOBAL FINANCIAL WARRIORS:
THE UNTOLD STORY OF INTERNATIONAL FINANCE
IN THE POST 9/11 WORLD

MONETARY POLICY RULES

HANDBOOK OF MACROECONOMICS
(with Michael Woodford)

INFLATION, UNEMPLOYMENT AND MONETARY POLICY
(with Robert Solow)

ECONOMICS
(with Akila Weerapana)

MACROECONOMIC POLICY IN A WORLD ECONOMY:
FROM ECONOMETRIC DESIGN TO PRACTICAL OPERATION

MACROECONOMICS:
THEORY, PERFORMANCE AND POLICY
(with Robert Hall)